Within The Words

Alexandra Diaz

Presentation by *BookLeaf Publishing*

Web: www.bookleafpub.com

E-mail: info@bookleafpub.com

ISBN: 9789357441568

First edition 2023

I really got into poetry when I was in sophomore year of high school. Then the more I wrote the more I wanted to become an author. I've been writing poetry for about 5 years.

Soul Mate

Their warmth becomes an addiction,
Their whispers become your drug.
Overdosing on love without anticipation.

Their arms become your safe haven,
Being secure that feeling is worth saving.
Making you feel appreciated, even on the days
you feel hated.

Their smile shine light on the darkest days,
Reminding you every flower needs rain.

Reflection

Let words people say and actions,
Make you flourish and blossom.
Use words to build your self esteem,
Like ammo to your gun.

You push and kept it all in, until it became
undone,
To prove what you can overcome.

Shoot the mirror in front of you,
That the haters have made.
Once it shatters so does the hate.

Pick up the pieces and build.
Take a breath, open your eyes to a new one, a
stronger you.
Which proved nothing can shatter you.

Sunset

Sitting on sand feeling the warm breeze on my
face,
Looking at the sky instantly feeling at peace.

Looking over the water seeing how far it
spreads,
Seeing the beauty of how the colors intertwine.
The light blues slowly turning into a soft pinkish
sky is a real gem to my eyes.

You don't want this moment to end but like the
days it will come again.
You will see it leave and see it come
That's the beauty of a sunset.

Future

You can't speak on something you don't know,
Don't be so anxious you might let it know.

The mysteries of the future is what has us on our feet,
Problems now don't mean defeat, just wait and see.

Be the best you now because the future isn't guaranteed,
So don't wait, appreciate whats in front of you.

You're present now, can be your future later.

Sea

It's so peaceful to see,
The sea can reel you in.
Like an anchor on a boat,
Or an arrow and a bow.

The feeling of the cold water beneath my feet,
Sending goosebumps all the way up to my
cheeks.
Looking up realizing the sea,
And the sky have similarities.

The further you go the harder it is to breathe,
But it worth the lung capacity.
As you swim, each stroke in the water,
Wraps around you giving warmth.

Paris

City of love, but with you it doesn't matter the
city,
Your smile shines brighter than the sky itself.
It's mesmerizing like the Eiffel Tower,
But that twinkle in your eyes is electrifying.

The city is alive, but so am I.
Sitting on your lap, whispering in your ear,
While you grab my thigh.

Paris is a place where you remember what love
is,
Not a city where only love exists.
You have to find it so let's begin!

Book

Each letter is a step we take in life.

A book is like make up on a face,
Judge too quickly, never get to see the inner
beauty.
If you pass, you won't see the beauty in the lines.
The lies between the lines or,
The truth that's hard to find.

Each chapter is a stage in your life,
Not everything's good, but there will always be a
climax.

A book is a journey with words and mind,
Your life can be one too, just make up your
mind.
A visual in your mind, by looking down at a
line,
Can give you a drive, just look between the
lines.

Fall

Inhaling the smell of oak trees,
Realizing finally the fall breeze.

How I missed the warm morning sun,
Chilly nights that make the hairs on my neck
stand up.
Warm pumpkin spice coffee warning up my
body,
The leave changing all around me.

Bon fires watching my reflection in the flames.
Seeing the stars twinkle in the midnight sky,
Finally my favorite season has arrived.

Heartless

Love can be more intoxicating than smoke in my
lungs.
Your smile was the keys in the ignition,
Your whispers is driving me on an endless road
to destruction.

I gave you my heart, you threw it away,
So I wonder was I ever good enough?
People try to be good and perfect, but no one
sees the real you as a person.

Urs sad how you can care si much that you lose
yourself,
And all they do is laugh, stabbing the truth in
your heart.

Remembering who you are is the key,
You may seem heartless, but it'll save you from
self destruction.

Lions

So beautiful, so enchanting yet so frightening,
Their golden mane glistening in the horizon.
Their eyes say stay away but,
Their souls is a little kid looking for a way out.

King of the jungle, fear strikes miles away,
others stay away when they hear your name.
So angry, so proud, yet no one knows the battles
you faced.

Forced to grow up, as he walked away, leaving
his family astray,
Becoming a father before you have any.
All your fears have to go away because the kings
of the jungle have no fear.

Seeds that Grow

Trees are beautiful sights; tall, strong facing the
sky,
Like a baby growing inside everything takes
time.

Every branch is a year of life, like when our hair
turns white.
Nourishment and care shows on how bright the
leaves shine,
Every foot is every step what's next only you can
assume.

It's a beautiful thing to know you made a
breathing thing that walks on earth.
Like one of the longest living things on earth, a
tree.

What if's

What if, what if
What if hellos are the new goodbyes?
What if you die before your time?
What if you get used to the lies?

So many things we don't know the answer to.
But why do you want to know?
The truth will eventually unfold.

Impatiences is our worst enemy,
Knowing before time can ruin the surprise!

Time

Time is endless, time isn't patient,
Time isn't forgetful, time is ambitious.
There will always be a deadline, doesn't matter if
it's finished.

There's all the time in the world yes, but for us
it's limited,
Can't wait until tomorrow to finish it.
What we learn today stays with us, hoping
tomorrow comes so we can use it unlimited.

Don't run away of the time running out,
Run free knowing nothing is holding you down.

Hostage

I am in prison and you are my prison guard,
I am in chained and you hold the key.

Butterflies in my stomach is overrated when it
comes to you.

You enslave my heart, making it ache,
Your presence makes my heart skip a beat.
Like I'm in for a real treat,
But I question if I'm free.

Your whispers cloud my judgement,
Your kissed are like poison to my lips.
Like a flower that smells too sweet.

Every step you take makes me grasp for air.
I close my eyes in you don't hear my heart,
throb like a hammer against cloth.

What's Perfect

Nothing in life is perfect.
People have expectations, have visions of a
future that isn't clear.
We must address and accept, and be happy with
what we get.

Living in regret is like living in debt.
Not truly living with content because something
is holding you back.
Sometimes you need to start fresh.

Scared to Live

I saw the pain in your eyes, wondering why,
Even thought we are together, you felt so alone.
Im sorry I've ruined your images of a happy life,
Because I know you wanted me by your side.

You are free, yet you still think of me.
Blaming me, cursing me, hating me,
Yet you are still glad to see me.

Don't be scared to live your life,
That I almost ruined for being selfish.

Sorry for the lies I even told myself,
I ignored the signs because you'll ask why.
In your eyes I can lie or love,
So I rather you move on.

Mirrors

Mirrors show our imperfections, up to us to
make them perfections,
Every piece of glass is like a cut in our veins,
forcing us to accept ourselves.

When you don't have a mirror, we can hide from
lies,
A mirror to your face Is like suicide to our eyes.
The shattered glass represents the broken pieces
to our heart, still trying to figure out the pieces
to the puzzle.

Bridges

Many tend to burn bridges, I say build them.

It's easy to destroy in fear of not knowing,
Take the first step, start with the stone you're
holding.
Vía versa the bridge can give you knowledge of
the unknowing.

The bridge is revealing itself, no time to waste,
The damage has been done, but who's to say it
can't be undone.
Don't be afraid, don't fade away,
It's here to heal and here to stay.

We move forward and never look back,
Let's enjoy the journey while it lasts.

Life

Instead of dreaming of a life you had,
Go and try it might not be so bad.
Don't be a victim of the past,
Be a product of your future.

Accept the past, live in the present, focus on the
future,
You might even surprise yourself.
Living is a choice, not an obligation,
Make it worth the blood in your veins, the
breaths you take.

Help

Help it only goes so far,
You have to learn the difference between
generosity and hypocrisy.

Some actually do want to see you excel, some
help yet hope you lose.

It's like a game of duck duck goose, they pick
and choose who they want to use.

It's Okay to Cry

It's okay to run, it's okay to hide,
It's okay to scream, it's okay to cry.

It's okay to have emotions you want to hide.
Avoid topics, hide your face made of glass,
Because one thrown pebble will have it turn to
Ashe.

Scream and shout until your tonsils wear out,
Break that frown that's been holding you down.
Being alone may be good at the moment.
But don't let a moment last a lifetime,
To the point where you forget how to laugh.